THE SOCIALIST ECONOMICS OF KARL MARX AND HIS FOLLOWERS

Thorstein Veblen

The Socialist Economics of Karl Marx and His Followers

Thorstein Veblen

The Quarterly Journal of Economics, volume 20, 1906.

I. The Theories of Karl Marx

The system of doctrines worked out by Marx is characterized by a certain boldness of conception and a great logical consistency. Taken in detail, the constituent elements of the system are neither novel nor iconoclastic, nor does Marx at any point claim to have discovered previously hidden facts or to have invented recondite formulations of facts already known; but the system as a whole has an air of originality and initiative such as is rarely met with among the sciences that deal with any phase of human culture. How much of this distinctive character the Marxian system owes to the personal traits of its creator is not easy to say, but what marks it off from all other systems of economic theory is not a matter of personal idiosyncrasy. It differs characteristically from all systems of theory that had preceded it, both in its premises and in its aims. The (hostile) critics of Marx have not sufficiently appreciated the radical character of his departure in both of these respects, and have, therefore, commonly lost themselves in a tangled scrutiny of supposedly abstruse details; whereas those writers who have been in sympathy with his teachings have too commonly been disciples bent on exegesis and on confirming their fellow-disciples in the faith.

Except as a whole and except in the light of its postulates and aims, the Marxian system is not only not tenable, but it is not even intelligible. A discussion of a given isolated feature of the system (such as the theory of value) from the point of view of classical economics (such as that offered by Bohm-Bawerk) is as futile as a discussion of solids in terms of two dimensions.

Neither as regards his postulates and preconceptions nor as regards the aim of his inquiry is Marx's position an altogether single-minded one In neither respect does his position come of a single line of antecedents. He is of no single school of philosophy, nor are his ideals those of any single group of speculators living before his time. For this reason he takes his place as an originator of a school of thought as well as the leader of a movement looking to a practical end.

As to the motives which drive him and the aspiration which guide him, in destructive criticism and an creative speculation alike, he is primarily a theoretician busied with the analysis of economic phenomena and their organization into a consistent and faithful system of scientific knowledge; but he is, at the same time, consistently and tenaciously alert to the bearing which each step in the progress of his theoretical work has upon the propaganda. His work has, therefore, an air of bias, such as belongs to an advocate's argument; but it is not, therefore, to be assumed, nor indeed to be credited, that his propagandist aims have in any substantial way deflected his inquiry or his speculations from the faithful pursuit of scientific truth. His socialistic bias may color his polemics, but his logical grasp is too neat and firm to admit of an bias, other than that of his metaphysical preconceptions, affecting his theoretical work.

There is no system of economic theory more logical than that of Marx. No member of the system, no single article of doctrine, is fairly to be understood, criticised, or defended except as an articulate member of the whole and in the light of the preconceptions and postulates which afford the point of departure and the controlling norm of the whole. As regards these preconceptions and postulates, Marx draws on two distinct lines of antecedents, -- the Materialistic Hegelianism and the English system of Natural Rights. By his earlier training he is an adept in the Hegelian method of speculation and inoculated with the metaphysics of development underlying the Hegelian system. By his later training he is an expert in the system of Natural Rights and Natural Liberty, ingrained in his ideals of life and held inviolate throughout. He does not take a critical attitude toward the underlying principles of Natural Rights. Even his Hegelian preconceptions of development never carry him the length of questioning the fundamental principles of that system. He is only more ruthlessly consistent in working out their content than his natural-rights antagonists in the liberal-classical school. His polemics run against the specific tenets of the liberal school, but they run wholly on the ground afforded by the premises of that school. The ideals of his propaganda are natural-rights ideals, but his theory of the working out of these ideals in the course of history rests on the Hegelian metaphysics of development, and his method of speculation and construction of theory is given by the Hegelian dialectic.

What first and most vividly centred interest on Marx and his speculations was his relation to the revolutionary socialistic movement; and it is those features of his doctrines which bear immediately on the propaganda that still continue to hold the attention of the greater number of his critics. Chief among these doctrines, in the apprehension of his critics, is the theory of value, with its corollaries: (a) the doctrines of the exploitation of labor by capital; and (b) the laborer's claim to the whole product of his labor. Avowedly, Marx traces his doctrine of labor value to Ricardo, and through him to the classical economists.2 The laborer's claim to the whole product of labor, which is pretty constantly implied, though not frequently avowed by Marx, he has in all probability taken from English writers of the early nineteenth century, 3 more particularly from William Thompson. These doctrines are, on their face, nothing but a development of the conceptions of natural rights which then pervaded English speculation and afforded the metaphysical ground of the liberal movement. The more formidable critics of the Marxian socialism have made much of these doctrinal elements that further the propaganda, and have, by laying the stress on these, diverted attention from other elements that are of more vital consequence to the system as a body of theory. Their exclusive interest in this side of "scientific socialism" has even led them to deny the Marxian system all substantial originality, and make it a (doubtfully legitimate) offshoot of English Liberalism and natural rights.4 But this is one-sided criticism. It may hold as against certain tenets of the so-called "scientific socialism," but it is not altogether to the point as regards the Marxian system of theory. Even the Marxian theory of value, surplus value, and exploitation, is not simply the doctrine of William Thompson, transcribed and sophisticated in a forbidding terminology, however great the superficial resemblance and however large Marx's unacknowledged debt to Thompson may be on these heads. For many details and for much of his animus Marx may be indebted to the Utilitarians; but, after all, his system of theory, taken as a whole, lies within the frontiers of neo-Hegelianism, and even the details are worked out in accord with the preconceptions of that school of thought and have taken on the completion that would properly belong to them on that ground. It is, therefore, not by an itemized scrutiny of the details of doctrine and by tracing their pedigree in detail that a fair conception of Marx and his contribution to economics may be reached, but rather by following him from his own point of departure out into the ramifications of his theory, and so overlooking the whole in the perspective which the lapse of time now affords us, but which he could not himself attain, since he was too near to his own work to see why he went about it as he did.

The comprehensive system of Marxism is comprised within the scheme of the Materialistic Conception of History.5 This materialistic conception is essentially Hegelian,6 although it belongs with the Hegelian Left, and its immediate affiliation is with Feuerbach, not with the direct line of Hegelian orthodoxy. The chief point of interest here, in identifying the materialistic conception with Hegelianism, is that this identification throws it immediately and uncompromisingly into contrast with Darwinism and the post-Darwinian conceptions of evolution. Even if a plausible English pedigree should be worked out for this Materialistic Conception, or "Scientific Socialism," as has been attempted, it remains none the less true that the conception with which Marx went to his work was a transmuted framework of Hegelian dialectic.7

Roughly, Hegelian materialism differs from Hegelian orthodoxy by inverting the main logical sequence, not by discarding the logic or resorting to new tests of truth or finality. One might say, though perhaps with excessive crudity, that, where Hegel pronounces his dictum, Das Denken ist das Sein, the materialists, particularly Marx and Engels, would say Das Sein macht das Denken. But in both cases some sort of a creative primacy is assigned to one or the other member of the complex, and in neither case is the relation between the two members a causal relation. In the materialistic conception man's spiritual life -- what man thinks -- is a reflex of what he is in the material respect, very much in the same fashion as the orthodox Hegelian would make the material world a reflex of the spirit. In both the dominant norm of speculation and formulation of theory is the conception of movement, development, evolution, progress; and in both the movement is contrived necessarily to take place by the method of conflict or struggle. The movement is of the nature of progress, -- gradual advance towards a goal, toward the realization in explicit form of all that is implicit in the substantial activity involved in the movement. The movement is, further, self-conditioned and self-acting: it is an unfolding by inner necessity. The struggle which constitutes the method of movement or evolution is, in the Hegelian system proper, the struggle of the spirit for self-realization by the process of the well-known three-phase dialectic. In the materialistic conception of history this dialectical movement becomes the class struggle of the Marxian system.

The class struggle is conceived to be "material," but the term "material" is in this connection used in a metaphorical sense. It does not mean mechanical or physical, or even physiological, but economic. It is material in the sense that it is a struggle between classes for the material means of life. "The materialistic conception of history proceeds on the principle that production and, next to production, the exchange of its products is the groundwork of every social order."8 The social order takes its form through the class struggle, and the character of the class struggle at any given phase of the unfolding development of society is determined by "the prevailing mode of economic production and exchange." The dialectic of the movement of social progress, therefore, moves on the spiritual plane of human desire and passion, not on the (literally) material plane of mechanical and physiological stress, on which the developmental process of brute creation unfolds itself. It is a sublimated materialism; sublimated by the dominating presence of the conscious human spirit; but it is conditioned by the material facts of the production of the means of life.9 The ultimately active forces involved in the process of unfolding social life are (apparently) the material agencies engaged in the mechanics of production; but the dialectic of the process - the class struggle - runs its course only among and in terms of the secondary (epigenetic) forces of human consciousness engaged in the valuation of the material products of industry. A consistently materialistic conception, consistently adhering to a materialistic interpretation of the process of development as well as of the facts involved in the process, could scarcely avoid making its putative dialectic struggle a mere unconscious and irrelevant conflict of the brute material forces. This would have amounted to an interpretation in terms of opaque cause and effect, without recourse to the concept of a conscious class struggle, and it might have led to a concept of evolution similar to the unteleological Darwinian concept of natural selection. It could scarcely have led to the Marxian notion of a conscious class struggle as the one necessary method of social progress, though it might conceivably, by the aid of empirical generalization, have led to a scheme of social process in which a class struggle would be included as an incidental though perhaps highly efficient factor.10 It would have led, as Darwinism has, to a concept of a process of cumulative change in social structure and function; but this process, being essentially a cumulative sequence of causation, opaque and unteleological, could not, without an infusion of pious fancy by the speculator be asserted to involve progress as distinct from retrogression or to tend to a "realization" or "self-realization" of the human spirit or of anything else. Neither could it conceivably be asserted to lead up to a final term, a goal to which all lines of the process should converge and beyond which the process would not go, such as the assumed goal of the Marxian process of class struggle which is conceived to cease in the classless economic structure of the socialistic final term. In Darwinianism there is no such final or perfect term, and no definitive equilibrium.

The disparity between Marxism and Darwinism, as well as the disparity within the Marxian system between the range of material facts that are conceived to be the fundamental forces of the process, on the one hand, and the range of spiritual facts within which the dialectical movement proceeds this disparity is shown in the character assigned the class struggle by Marx and Engels. The struggle is asserted to be a conscious one, and proceeds On a recognItion by the competing classes of their mutually incompatible interests with regard to the material means of life. The class struggle proceeds on motives of interest, and a recognition of class interest can, of course, be reached only by reflection on the facts of the case. There is, therefore, not even a dIrect causal connection between the material forces in the case and the choice of a given interested line of conduct. The attitude of the interested party does not result from the material forces so immediately as to place it within the relation of direct cause and effect, nor even with such a degree of intimacy as to admit of its being classed as a tropismatic, or even instinctive, response to the impact of the material force in question. The sequence of reflection, and the consequent choice of sides to a quarrel, run entirely alongside of the range of material facts concerned.

A further characteristic of the doctrine of class struggle requires mention. While the concept is not Darwinian, it is also not legitimately Hegelian, whether of the Right or the Left. It is of a utilitarian origin and of English pedigree, and it belongs to Marx by virtue of his having borrowed its elements from the system of self-interest. It is in fact a piece of hedonism, and is related to Bentham rather than to Hegel. It proceeds on the grounds of the hedonistic calculus, which is equally foreign to the Hegelian notion of an unfolding process and to the post-Darwinian notions of cumulative causation. As regards the tenability of the doctrine, apart from the question of its derivation and its compatibility with the neo-Hegelian postulates, it is to be added that it is quite out of harmony with the later results of psychological inquiry, just as is true of the use made of the hedonistic calculus by the classical (Austrian) economics.

Within the domain covered by the materialistic conception, that is to say within the domain of unfolding human culture, which is the field of Marxian speculation at large, Marx has more particularly devoted his efforts to an analysis and theoretical formulation of the present situation, -- the current phase of the process, the capitalistic system. And, since the prevailing mode of the production of goods determines the institutional, intellectual, and spiritual life of the epoch, by determining the form and method of the current class struggle, the discussion necessarily begins with the theory of "capitalistic production," or production as carried on under the capitalistic system.11 Under the capitalistic system, that is to say under the system of modern business traffic, production is a production of commodities, merchantable goods, with a view to the price to be obtained for them in the market. The great fact on which all industry under this system hinges is the price of marketable goods. Therefore it is at this point that Marx strikes into the system of capitalistic production, and therefore the theory of value becomes the dominant feature of his economics and the point of departure for the whole analysis, in all its voluminous ramifications.12

It is scarcely worth while to question what serves as the beginning of wisdom in the current criticisms of Marx; namely, that he offers no adequate proof of his labor-value theory.13 It is even safe to go further, and say that he offers no proof of it. The feint which occupies the opening paragraphs of the Kapital and the corresponding passages of Zur Kritik, etc., is not to be taken seriously as an attempt to prove his position on this head by the ordinary recourse to argument. It is rather a self-satisfied superior's playful mystification of those readers (critics) whose limited powers do not enable them to see that his proposition is self-evident. Taken on the Hegelian (neo-Hegelian) ground, and seen in the light of the general materialistic conception, the proposition that value -- labor-cost is self-evident, not to say tautological. Seen in any other light, it has no particular force.

In the Hegelian scheme of things the only substantial reality is the unfolding life of the spirit. In the neo-Hegelian scheme, as embodied in the materialistic conception, this reality is translated into terms of the unfolding (material) life of man in society.14 In so far as the goods are products of industry, they are the output of this unfolding life of man, a material residue embodying a given fraction of this forceful life process. In this life process lies all substantial reality, and all finally valid relations of quantivalence between the products of this life process must run in its terms. The life process, which, when it takes the specific form of an expenditure of labor power, goes to produce goods, is a process of material forces, the spiritual or mental features of the life process and of labor being only its insubstantial reflex. It is consequently only in the material changes wrought by this expenditure of labor power that the metaphysical substance of life - labor power - can be embodied; but in these changes of material fact it cannot but be embodied, since these are the end to which it is directed.

This balance between goods in respect of their magnitude as output of human labor holds good indefeasibly, in point of the metaphysical reality of the life process, whatever superficial (phenomenal) variations from this norm may occur in men's dealings with the goods under the stress of the strategy of self-interest. Such is the value of the goods in reality; they are equivalents of one another in the proportion in which they partake of this substantial quality, although their true ratio of equivalence may never come to an adequate expression in the transactions involved in the distribution of the goods. This real or true value of the goods is a fact of production, and holds true under all systems and methods of production, whereas the exchange value (the "phenomenal form" of the real value) is a fact of distribution, and expresses the real value more or less adequately according as the scheme of distribution force at the given time conforms more or less closely to the equities given by production. If the output of industry were distributed to the productive agents strictly in proportion to their shares in production, the exchange value of the goods would be presumed to conform to their real value. But, under the current, capitalistic system, distribution is not in any sensible degree based on the equities of production, and the exchange value of goods under this system can therefore express their real value only with a very rough, and in the main fortuitous, approximation. Under a socialistic rááágime, where the laborer would get the full product of his labor, or where the whole system of ownership, and consequently the system of distribution, would lapse, values would reach a true expression, if any.

Under the capitalistic system the determination of exchange value is a matter of competitive profit-making, and exchange values therefore depart erratically and incontinently from the proportions that would legitimately be given them by the real values whose only expression they are. Marx's critics commonly identify the concept of "value" with that of "exchange value," 15 and show that the theory of "value" does not square with the run of the facts of price under the existing system of distribution, piously hoping thereby to have refuted the Marxian doctrine; whereas, of course, they have for the most part not touched it. The misapprehension of the critics may be due to a (possibly intentional) oracular obscurity on the part of Marx. Whether by his fault or their own, their refutations have hitherto been quite inconclusive. Marx's severest stricture on the iniquities of the capitalistic system is that contained by implication in his development of the manner in which actual exchange value of goods systematically diverges from their real (labor-cost) value.

Herein, indeed, lies not only the Inherent iniquity of the existing system, but also its fateful infirmity, according to Marx.

The theory of value, then, is contained in the main postulates of the Marxian system rather than derived from them. Marx identifies this doctrine, in its elements, with the labor-value theory of Ricardo,16 but the relationship between the two is that of a superficial coincidence in their main propositions rather than a substantial identity of theoretic contents. In Ricardo's theory the source and measure of value is sought in the effort and sacrifice undergone by the producer, consistently, on the whole, with the Benthamite-utilitarian position to which Ricardo somewhat loosely and uncritically adhered. The decisive fact about labor, that quality by virtue of which it is assumed to be the final term in the theory of production, is its irksomeness. Such is of course not the case in the labor-value theory of Marx, to whom the question of the irksomeness of labor is quite irrelevant, so far as regards the relation between labor and production. The substantial diversity or incompatibility of the two theories shows itself directly when each is employed by its creator in the further analysis of economic phenomena. Since with Ricardo the crucial point is the degree of irksomeness of labor, which serves as a measure both of the labor expended and the value produced, and since in Ricardo's utilitarian philosophy there is no more vital fact underlying this irksomeness, therefore no surplus-value theory follows from the main position. The productiveness of labor is not cumulative. in its own working; and the Ricardian economics goes on to seek the cumulative productiveness of industry in the functioning of the products of labor when employed in further production and in the irksomeness of the capitalist's abstinence. From which duly follows the general position of classical economics on the theory of production.

With Marx, on the other hand, the labor power expended in production being itself a product and having a substantial value corresponding to its own labor cost, the value of the labor power expended and the value of the product created by its expenditure need not be the same. They are not the same, by supposition, as they would be in any hedonistic interpretation of the facts. Hence a discrepancy arises between the value of the labor power expended in production and the value of the product created, and this discrepancy is covered by the concept of surplus value. Under the capitalistic system, wages being the value (price) of the labor power consumed in industry, it follows that the surplus product of their labor cannot go to the laborers, but becomes the profits of capital and the source of its accumulation and increase. From the fact that wages are measured by the value of labor power rather than by the (greater) value of the product of labor , it follows also that the laborers are unable to buy the whole product of their labor, and so that the capitalists are unable to sell the whole product of industry continuously at its full value, whence arise difficulties of the gravest nature in the capitalistic system, in the way of overproduction and the like.

But the gravest outcome of this systematic discrepancy between the value of labor power and the value of its product is the accumulation of capital out of unpaid labor and the effect of this accumulation on the laboring population. The law of accumulation, with its corollary, the doctrine of the industrial reserve army, is the final term and the objective point of Marx's theory of capitalist production, just as the theory of labor value is his point of departure.17 While the theory of value and surplus value are Marx's explanation of the possibility of existence of the capitalistic system, the law of the accumulation of capital is his exposition of the causes which must lead to the collapse of that system and of the manner in which the collapse will come. And since Marx is, always and everywhere, a socialist agitator as well as a theoretical economist, it may be said without hesitation that the law of accumulation is the climax of his great work, from whatever point of view it is looked at, whether as an economic theorem or as a tenet of socialistic doctrine.

The law of capitalistic accumulation may be paraphrased as follows:18 Wages being the (approximately exact) value of the labor power bought in the wage contract; the price of the product being the (similarly approximate) value of the goods produced; and since the value of the product exceeds that of the labor power by a given amount (surplus value), which by force of the wage contract passes into the possession of the capitalist and is by him in part laid by as savings and added to the capital already in hand, it follows (a) that, other things equal, the larger the surplus value, the more rapid the increase of capital; and also (b), that the greater the increase of capital relatively to the labor force employed, the more productive the labor employed and the larger the surplus product available for accumulation. The process of accumulation, therefore, is evidently a cumulative one; and, also evidently, the increase added to capital is an unearned increment drawn from the unpaid surplus product of labor.

But with an appreciable increase of the aggregate capital a change takes place in its technological composition, whereby the "constant" capital (equipment and raw materials) increases disproportionately as compared with the "variable" capital (wages fund). "Labor-saving devices" are used to a greater extent than before, and labor is saved. A larger proportion of the expenses of production goes for the purchase of equipment and raw materials, and a smaller proportion -- though perhaps an absolutely increased amount - goes for the purchase of labor power. Less labor is needed relatively to the aggregate capital employed as well as relatively to the quantity of goods produced. Hence some portion of the increasing labor supply will not be wanted, and an "industrial reserve army," a "surplus labor population," an army of unemployed, comes into existence. This reserve grows relatively larger as the accumulation of capital proceeds and as technological improvements consequently gain ground ; so that there result two divergent cumulative changes in the situation, -- antagonistic, but due to the same set of forces and, therefore, inseparable: capital increases, and the number of unemployed laborers (relatively) increases also.

This divergence between the amount of capital and output, on the one hand, and the amount received by laborers as wages, on the other hand, has an incidental consequence of some importance. The purchasing power of the laborers, represented by their wages, being the largest part of the demand for consumable goods, and being at the same time, in the nature of the case, progressively less adequate for the purchase of the product, represented by the price of the goods produced, it follows that the market is progressively more subject to glut from overproduction, and hence to commercial crises and depression. It has been argued, as if it were a direct inference from Marx's position, that this maladjustment between production and markets, due to the laborer not getting the full product of his labor, leads directly to the breakdown of the capitalistic system, and so by its own force will bring on the socialistic consummation. Such is not Marx's position, however, although crises and depression play an important part in the course of development that is to lead up to socialism. In Marx's theory, socialism is to come by way of a conscious class movement on the part of the propertyless laborers, who will act advisedly on their own interest and force the revolutionary movement for their own gain. But crises and depression will have a large share in bringing the laborers to a frame of mind suitable for such a move.

Given a growing aggregate capital, as indicated above, and a concomitant reserve of unemployed laborers growing at a still higher rate, as is involved in Marx's position, this body of unemployed labor can be, and will be, used by the capitalists to depress wages, in order to increase profits. Logically, it follows that, the farther and faster capital accumulates, the larger will be the reserve of unemployed, both absolutely and relatively to the work to be done, and the more severe will be the pressure acting to reduce wages and lower the standard of living, and the deeper will be the degradation and misery of the working class and the more precipitately will their condition decline to a still lower depth. Every period of depression, with its increased body of unemployed labor seeking work, will act to hasten and accentuate the depression of wages, until there is no warrant even for holding that wages will, on an average, be kept up to the subsistence minimum.19 Marx, indeed, is explicit to the effect that such will be the case, that wages will decline below the subsistence minimum; and he cites English conditions of child labor, misery, and degeneration to substantiate his views.20 When this has gone far enough, when capitalist production comes near enough to occupying the whole field of industry and has depressed the condition of its laborers sufficiently to make them an effective majority of the community with nothing to lose, then, having taken advice together, they will move, by legal or extra-legal means, by absorbing the state or by subverting it, to establish the social revolution, Socialism is to come through class antagonism due to the absence of all property interests from the laboring class, coupled with a generally prevalent misery so profound as to involve some degree of physical degeneration. This misery is to be brought about by the heightened productivity of labor due to an increased accumulation of capital and large improvements in the industrial arts; which in turn is caused by the fact that under a system of private enterprise with hired labor the laborer does not get the whole product of his labor; which, again, is only saying in other words that private ownership of capital goods enables the capitalist to appropriate and accumulate the surplus product of labor. As to what the régime is to be which the social revolution will bring in, Marx has nothing particular to say beyond the general thesis that there will be no private ownership, at least not of the means of production.

Such are the outlines of the Marxian system of socialism, In all that has been said so far no recourse is had to the second and third volumes of Kapital. Nor is it necessary to resort to these two volumes for the general theory of socialism. They add nothing essential, although many of the details of the processes concerned in the working out of the capitalist scheme are treated with greater fulness, and the analysis is carried out with great consistency and with admirable results. For economic theory at large these further two volumes are important enough, but an inquiry into their contents in that connection is not called for here.

Nothing much need be said as to the tenability of this theory. In its essentials, or at least in its characteristic elements, it has for the most part been given up by latterday socialist writers. The number of those who hold to it without essential deviation is growing gradually smaller. Such is necessarily the case, and for more than one reason. The facts are not bearing it out on certain critical points, such as the doctrine of increasing misery; and the Hegelian philosophical postulates, without which the Marxism of Marx is groundless, are for the most part forgotten by the dogmatists of to-day. Darwinism has largely supplanted Hegelianism in their habits of thought.

The particular point at which the theory is most fragile, considered simply as a theory of social growth, is its implied doctrine of population, implied in the doctrine of a growing reserve of unemployed workmen. The doctrine of the reserve of unemployed labor involves as a postulate that population will increase anyway, without reference to current or prospective means of life. The empirical facts give at least a very persuasive apparent support to the view expressed by Marx, that misery is, or has hitherto been, no hindrance to the propagation of the race; but they afford no conclusive evidence in support of a thesis to the effect that the number of laborers must increase independently of an increase of the means of life. No one since Darwin would have the hardihood to say that the increase of the human species is not conditioned by the means of living.

But all that does not really touch Marx's position. To Marx, the neo-Hegelian, history, including the economic development, is the life-history of the human species; and the main fact in this life-history, particularly in the economic aspect of it, is the growing volume of human life. This, in a manner of speaking, is the base-line of the whole analysis of the process of economic life, including the phase of capitalist production with the rest.

The growth of population is the first principle, the most substantial, most material factor in this process of economic life, so long as it is a process of growth, of unfolding, of exfoliation, and not a phase of decrepitude and decay. Had Marx found that his analysis led him to a view adverse to this position, he would logically have held that the capitalist system is the mortal agony of the race and the manner of its taking off. Such a conclusion is precluded by his Hegelian point of departure, according to which the goal of the life-history of the race in a large way controls the course of that life-history in all its phases, including the phase of capitalism. This goal or end, which controls the process of human development, is the complete realization of life in all its fulness, and the realization is to be reached by a process analogous to the three-phase dialectic, of thesis, antithesis, and synthesis, into which scheme the capitalist system, with its overflowing measure of misery and degradation, fits as the last and most dreadful phase of antithesis. Marx, as a Hegelian, -- that is to say, a romantic philosopher, -- is necessarily an optimist, and the evil (antithetical element) in life is to him a logically necessary evil, as the antithesis is a necessary phase of the dialectic; and it is a means to the consummation, as the antithesis is a means to the synthesis.

Notes

1. The substance of lectures before students in Harvard University in April, 1906.

2. Cf. Critique of Political Economy, chap. i, "Notes on the History of the Theory of Commodities," pp. 56-73 (English translation, New York, 1904).

3. See Menger, Right to the Whole Produce of Labor, section iii-v and viii-ix, and Foxwell's admirable Introduction to Menger.

4. See Menger and Foxwell, as above, and Schaeffle, Quintessence of Socialism, and The Impossibility or Social Democracy.

5. See Engels, The Development of Socialism from Utopia to Science, especially section ii. and the opening paragraphs of section iii.; also the preface of Zur Kritik der politischen Oekonomie.

6. See Engels, as above, and also his Feuerbach: The Roots of Socialist Philosophy (translation, Chicago, Kerr & Co., 1903).

7. See, e.g., Seligman, The Economic Interpretation of History, Part I.

8. Engels, Development of Socialism, beginning of section iii.

9. Cf., on this point, Max Adler, "Kausalitat und Teleologie in Streite um die Wissenschaft" (included in Marx -- Studien, edited by Adler and Hilfendirg, vol. i), particularly section xi; cf. also Ludwig Stein, Die soziale Frage im Lichte der Philosophie, whom Adler criticizes and claims to have refuted.

10. Cf., Alder as above.

11. It may be noted, by way of caution to readers familiar with the terms only as employed by the classical (English and Austrian) economists, that in Marxian usage "capitalistic production" means production of goods for the market by hired labor under the direction of employers who own (or control) the means of production and are engaged in industry for the sake of profit. "Capital" is wealth (primarily funds) so employed. In these and other related points of terminological usage Marx is, of course, much more in touch with colloquial usage than those economists of the classical line who make capital signify "the products of past industry used as aids to further production." With Marx "Capitalism" implies certain relations of ownership, no less than the "productive use" which is alone insisted on by so many later economists in defining the term.

12. In the sense that the theory of value affords the point of departure and the fundamental concepts out of which the further theory of the workings of capitalism is constructed, -- in this sense, and in this sense only, is the theory of value the central doctrine and the critical tenet of Marxism. It does not follow that Marxist doctrine of an irresistible drift towards a socialistic consummation hangs on the defensibility of the labor-value theory, nor even that the general structure of the Marxist economics would collapse if translated into other terms than those of this doctrine of labor value. Cf. Bohm-Bawerk, Karl Marx and the Close of his System; and, on the other hand, Frans

Oppenheimer, Das Grundgesetz der Marx'schen Gesellschaftslehre, and Rudolf Goldscheid, Verelendungs -- oder Meliorationstheorie.

13. Cf., e.g., Bohm-Bawerk, as above; Georg Adler, Grundlagen der Karl Marx'schen Kritik.

14. In much the same way, and with an analogous effect on their theoretical work, in the preconceptions of the classical (including the Austrian) economists, the balance of pleasure and pain is taken to be the ultimate reality in terms of which all economic theory must be stated and to terms of which all phenomena should finally be reduced in any definitive analysis of economic life. It is not the present purpose to inquire whether the one of these uncritical assumptions is in any degree more meritorious or more serviceable than the other.

15. Bohm-Bawerk, Capital and Interest, Book VI, chap. iii; also Karl Marx and the Close of his System, particularly chap. iv; Adler, Grundlagen, chaps. ii and iii

16. Cf. Kapital, vol. i, chap. xv, p.486 (4th ed.). See also notes 9 and 16 to chap. i of the same volume, where Marx discusses the labor-value doctrines of Adam Smith and an earlier (anonymous) English writer and compares them with his own. Similar comparisons with the early -- Classical -- value theories recur from time to time in the later portions of Kapital.

17. Oppenheimer (Das Grundgesertz der Marx'schen Gesellschaftslehre) is right in making the theory of accumulation the central element in the doctrines of Marxist socialism, but it does not follow, as Oppenheimer contends, that this doctrine is the keystone of Marx's economic theories. It follows logically from the theory of surplus value, as indicated above, and rests on that theory in such a way that it would fail (in the form in which it is held by Marx) with the failure of the doctrine of surplus value.

18. See Kapital, vol. i, chap. xxiii.

19. The "subsistence minimum" is here taken in the sense used by Marx and the classical economists, as meaning what is necessary to keep up the supply of labor at its current rate of efficiency.

20. See Kapital, vol. i, chap. xxiii, sections 4 and 5.

II. The Later Marxism

The substance of lectures before students in Harvard University in April, 1906.

Marx worked out his system of theory in the main during the third quarter of the nineteenth century. He came to the work from the standpoint given him by his early training in German thought, such as the most advanced and aggressive German thinking was through the middle period of the century, and he added to this German standpoint the further premises given him by an exceptionally close contact with and alert observation of the

English situation. The result is that he brings to his theoretical work a twofold line of premises, or rather of preconceptions. By early training he is a neo-Hegelian, and from this German source he derives his peculiar formulation of the Materialistic Theory of History. By later experience he acquired the point of view of that Liberal-Utilitarian school which dominated English thought through the greater part of his active life. To this experience he owes (probably) the somewhat pronounced individualistic preconceptions on which the doctrines of the Full Product of Labor and the Exploitation of Labor are based. These two not altogether compatible lines of doctrine found their way together into the tenets of scientific 1 socialism, and give its characteristic Marxian features to the body of socialist economics.

The socialism that inspires hopes and fears to-day is of the school of Marx. No one is seriously apprehensive of any other so-called socialistic movement, and no one is seriously concerned to criticise or refute the doctrines set forth by any other school of "socialists." It may be that the socialists of Marxist observance are not always or at all points in consonance with the best accepted body of Marxist doctrine. Those who make up the body of the movement may not always be familiar with the details perhaps not even with the general features -- of the Marxian scheme of economics; but with such consistency as may fairly be looked for in any popular movements the socialists of all countries gravitate toward the theoretical position of the avowed Marxism. In proportion as the movement in any given community grows in mass, maturity, and conscious purpose, it unavoidably takes on a more consistently Marxian complexion. It is not the Marxism of Marx, but the materialism of Darwin, which the socialists of today have adopted. The Marxist socialists of Germany have the lead, and the socialists of other countries largely take their cue from the German leaders.

The authentic spokesmen of the current international socialism are avowed Marxists. Exceptions to that rule are very few. On the whole, substantial truth of the Marxist doctrines is not seriously questioned within the lines of the socialists, tho there may be some appreciable divergence as to what the true Marxist position is on one point and another. Much and eager controversy circles about questions of that class.

The keepers of the socialist doctrines are passably agreed as to the main position and the general principles. Indeed, so secure is this current agreement on the general principles that a very lively controversy on matters of detail may go on without risk of disturbing the general position. This general position is avowedly Marxism. But it is not precisely the position held by Karl Marx. It has been modernized, adapted, tilled out, in response to exigencies of a later date than those which conditioned the original formulation of the theories. It is, of course, not admitted by the followers of Marx that any substantial change or departure from the original position has taken place. They are somewhat jealously orthodox, and are impatient of any suggested "improvements" on the Marxist position, as witness the heat engendered in the "revisionist" controversy of a few years back. But the jealous protests of the followers of Marx do not alter the fact that Marxism has undergone some substantial change since it left the hands of its creator. Now and then a more or less consistent disciple of Marx will avow a need of adapting the received doctrines to circumstances that have arisen later than the formulation of the doctrines; and amendments, qualifications, and extensions, with this need in view, have been offered from time to time. But more pervasive tho unavowed changes have come in the teachings of Marxism by way of interpretation and an unintended shifting of the point of view. Virtually, the whole of the younger generation of socialist writers shows such a growth. A citation of personal instances would be quite futile.

It is the testimony of his friends as well as of his writings that the theoretical position of Marx, both as regards his standpoint and as regards his main tenets, fell into a definitive shape relatively early, and that his later work was substantially a working out of what was contained in the position taken at the outset of his career.2 By the latter half of the forties, if not by the middle of the forties, Marx and Engels had found the outlook on human life which came to serve as the point of departure and the guide for their subsequent development of theory. Such is the view of the matter expressed by Engels during the later years of his life.3 The position taken by the two greater leaders, and held by them substantially intact, was a variant of neo-Hegelianism, as has been indicated in an earlier section of this paper.4 But neo-Hegelianism was short-lived, particularly considered as a standpoint for scientific theory. The whole romantic school of thought, comprising neo-Hegelianism with the rest, began to go to pieces very soon after it had reached an approach to maturity, and its disintegration proceeded with exceptional speed, so that the close of the third quarter of the century saw the virtual end of it as a vital factor in the development of human knowledge. In the realm of theory, primarily of course in the material sciences, the new era belongs not to romantic philosophy, but to the evolutionists of the school of Darwin. Some few great figures, of course, stood over from the earlier days, but it turns out in the sequel that they have served mainly to mark the rate and degree in which the method of scientific knowledge has left them behind. Such were Virchow and Max Muller, and such, in economic science, were the great figures of the Historical School, and such, in a degree, were also Marx and Engels. The later generation of socialists, the spokesmen and adherents of Marxism during the closing quarter of the century, belong to the new generation, and see the phenomena of human life under the new light. The materialistic conception in their handling of it takes on the color of the time in which they lived, even while they retain the phraseology of the generation that went before them.5 The difference between the romantic school of thought, to which Marx belonged, and the school of the evolutionists into whose hands the system has fallen, -- or perhaps, better, is falling, -- is great and pervading, tho it may not show a staring superficial difference at any one point, - at least not yet. The discrepancy between the two is likely to appear more palpable and more sweeping when the new method of knowledge has been applied with fuller realization of its reach and its requirements in that domain of knowledge that once belonged to the neo-Hegelian Marxism. The supplanting of the one by the other has been taking place slowly, gently, in large measure unavowedly, by a sort of precession of the point of view from which men size up the facts and reduce them to intelligible order.

The neo-Hegelian, romantic, Marxian standpoint was wholly personal, whereas the evolutionistic -- it may be called Darwinian -- standpoint is wholly impersonal. The continuity sought in the facts of observation and imputed to them by the earlier school of theory was a continuity of a personal kind, -- a continuity of reason and consequently of logic. The facts were construed to take such a course as could be established by an appeal to reason between intelligent and fair-minded men. They were supposed to fall into a sequence of logical consistency. The romantic (Marxian) sequence of theory is essentially an intellectual sequence, and it is therefore of a teleological character. The logical trend of it can be argued out. That is to say, it tends to a goal. It must eventuate in a consummation, a final term. On the other hand, in the Darwinian scheme of thought, the continuity sought in and imputed to the facts is a continuity of cause and effect. It is a scheme of blindly cumulative causation, in which there is no trend, no final term, no consummation. The sequence is controlled by nothing but the vis a tergo of brute causation, and is essentially mechanical. The neo-Hegelian (Marxian) scheme of development is drawn in the image of the struggling ambitious human spirit: that of Darwinian evolution is of the nature of a mechanical process.6

What difference, now, does it make if the materialistic conception is translated from the romantic concepts of Marx into the mechanical concepts of Darwinism? It distorts every feature of the system in some degree, and throws a shadow of doubt on every conclusion that once seemed secure.7 The first principle of the Marxian scheme is the concept covered by the term "Materialistic," to the effect that the exigencies of the material means of life control the conduct of men in society throughout, and thereby indefeasibly guide the growth of institutions and shape every shifting trait of human culture. This control of the life of society by the material exigencies takes effect thru men's taking thought of material (economic) advantages and disadvantages, and choosing that which will yield the iller material measure of life. When the materialistic conception passes under the Darwinian norm, of cumulative causation, it happens, first, that this initial principle itself is reduced to the rank of a habit of thought induced in the speculator who depends on its light by the circumstances of his life, in the way of hereditary bent, occupation, tradition, education, climate, food supply, and the like. But under the Darwinian norm the question of whether and how far material exigencies control human conduct and cultural growth becomes a question of the share which these material exigencies have in shaping men's habits of thought; i.e., their ideals and aspirations, their sense of the true, the beautiful, and the good. Whether and how far these traits of human culture and the institutional structure built out of them are the outgrowth of material (economic) exigencies becomes a question of what kind and degree of efficiency belongs to the economic exigencies among the complex of circumstances that conduce to the formation of habits. It is no longer a question of whether material exigencies rationally should guide men's conduct, but whether, as a matter of brute causation, they do induce such habits of thought in men as the economic interpretation presumes, and whether in the last analysis economic exigencies alone are, directly or indirectly, effective in shaping human habits of thought.

Tentatively and by way of approximation some such formulation as that outlined in the last paragraph is apparently what Bernstein and others of the "revisionists" have been seeking in certain of their speculations,8 and, sitting austere and sufficient on a dry shoal up stream, Kautsky has uncomprehendingly been addressing them advice and admonition which they do not understand.9 The more intelligent and enterprising among the idealist wing - where intellectual enterprise is not a particularly obvious trait have been struggling to speak for the view that the forces of the environment may effectually reach men's spiritual life thru other avenues than the calculus of the main chance, and so may give rise to habitual ideals and aspirations independent of, and possibly alien to, that calculus.10

So, again, as to the doctrine of the class struggle. In the Marxian scheme of dialectical evolution the development which is in this way held to be controlled by the material exigencies must, it is held, proceed by the method of the class struggle. This class struggle is held to be inevitable, and is held inevitably to lead at each revolutionary epoch to a more efficient adjustment of human industry to human uses, because. when a large proportion of the community find themselves ill served by the current economic arrangements, they take thought, band together, and enforce a readjustment more equitable and more advantageous to them. So long as differences of economic advantage prevail, there will be a divergence of interests between those more advantageously placed and those less advantageously placed. The members of society will take sides as this line of cleavage indicated by their several economic interests may decide. Class solidarity will arise on the basis of this class interest, and a struggle between the two classes so marked off against each other will set in, -- a struggle which, in the logic of the situation, can end only when the previously less fortunate class gains the ascendency, -- and so must the class struggle proceed until it shall have put an end to that diversity of economic interest on which the class struggle rests. All this is logically consistent and convincing, but it proceeds on the ground of reasoned conduct, calculus of advantage, not on the ground of cause and effect. The class struggle so conceived should always and everywhere tend unremittingly toward the socialistic consummation, and should reach that consummation in the end, whatever obstructions or diversions might retard the sequence of development along the way. Such is the notion of it embodied in the system of Marx. Such, however, is not the showing of history. Not all nations or civilizations have advanced unremittingly toward a socialistic consummation, in which all divergence of economic interest has lapsed or would lapse. Those nations and civilizations which have decayed and failed, as nearly all known nations and civilizations have done, illustrate the point that, however reasonable and logical the advance by means of the class struggle may be, it is by no means inevitable. Under the Darwinian norm it must be held that men's reasoning is largely controlled by other than logical, intellectual forces; that the conclusion reached by public or class opinion is as much, or more, a matter of sentiment than of logical inference; and that the sentiment which animates men, singly or collectively, is as much, or more, an outcome of habit and native propensity as of calculated material interest. There is, for instance, no warrant in the Darwinian scheme of things for asserting a priori that the class interest of the working class will bring them to take a stand against the propertied class. It may as well be that their training in subservience to their employers will bring them again to realize the equity and excellence of the established system of subjection and unequal distribution of wealth. Again, no one, for instance, can tell to-day what will be the outcome of the present situation in Europe and America. It may be that the working classes will go forward along the line of the socialistic ideals and enforce a new deal, in which there shall be no economic class discrepancies, no international animosity, no dynastic politics.

But then it may also, so far as can be foreseen, equally well happen that the working class, with the rest of the community in Germany, England, or America, will be led by the habit of loyalty and by their sportsmanlike propensities to lend themselves enthusiastically to the game of drastic politics which alone their sportsmanlike rulers consider worth while. It is quite impossible on Darwinian ground to foretell whether the "proletariat" will go on to establish the socialistic revolution or turn aside again, and sink their force in the broad sands of patriotism. It is a question of habit and native propensity and of the range of stimuli to which the proletariat are exposed and are to be exposed, and what may be the outcome is not a matter of logical consistency, but of response to stimulus.

So, then, since Darwinian concepts have begun to dominate the thinking of the Marxists, doubts have now and again come to assert themselves both as to the inevitableness of the irrepressible class struggle and to its sole efficacy. Anything like a violent class struggle, a seizure of power by force, is more and more consistently deprecated. For resort to force, it is felt, brings in its train coercive control with all its apparatus of prerogative, mastery, and subservience.11

So, again, the Marxian doctrine of progressive proletarian distress, the so-called Verelendungstheorie, which stands pat on the romantic ground of the original Marxism, has fallen into abeyance, if not into disrepute, since the Darwinian conceptions have come to prevail. As a matter of reasoned procedure, on the ground of enlightened material interest alone, it should be a tenable position that increasing misery, increasing in degree and in volume, should be the outcome of the present system of ownership; and should at the same time result in a well-advised and well-consolidated working-class movement that would replace the present system by a scheme more advantageous to the majority. But so soon as the question is approached on the Darwinian ground of cause and effect, and is analyzed in terms of habit and of response to stimulus, the doctrine that progressive misery must effect a socialistic revolution becomes dubious, and very shortly untenable. Experience, the experience of history, teaches that abject misery carries with it deterioration and abject subjection. The theory of progressive distress fits convincingly into the scheme of the Hegelian three-phase dialectic. It stands for the antithesis that is to be merged in the ulterior synthesis; but it has no particular force on the ground of an argument from cause to effect.12

It fares not much better with the Marxian theory of value and its corollaries and dependent doctrines when Darwinian concepts are brought in to replace the romantic elements out of which it is built up. Its foundation is the metaphysical equality between the volume of human life force productively spent in the making of goods and the magnitude of these goods considered as human products. The question of such an equality has no meaning in terms of cause and effect, nor does it bear in any intelligible way upon the Darwinian question of the fitness of any given system of production or distribution. In any evolutionary system of economics the central question touching the efficiency and fitness of any given system of production is necessarily the question as to the excess of serviceability in the product over the cost of production.13 It is in such an excess of serviceability over cost that the chance of survival lies for any system of production, in so far as the question of survival is a question of production, and this matter comes into the speculation of Marx only indirectly or incidentally, and leads to nothing in his argument.

And, as bearing on the Marxian doctrines of exploitation, there is on Darwinian ground no place for a natural right to the full product of labor. What can be argued in that connection on the ground of cause and effect simply is the question as to what scheme of distribution will help or hinder the survival of a given people or a given civilization.14 But these questions of abstruse theory need not be pursued, since they count, after all, but relatively little among the working tenets of the movement. Little need be done by the Marxists to work out or to adapt the Marxian system of value theory, since it has but slight bearing on the main question, -- the question of the trend towards socialism and of its chances of success. It is conceivable that a competent theory of value dealing with the excess of serviceability over cost, on the one hand, and with the discrepancy between price and serviceability, on the other hand, would have a substantial bearing upon the advisability of the present as against the socialistic rááágime, and would go far to clear up the notions of both socialists and conservatives as to the nature of the points in dispute between them.

But the socialists have not moved in the direction of this problem, and they have the excuse that their critics have suggested neither a question nor a solution to a question along any such line. None of the value theorists have so far offered anything that could be called good, bad, or indifferent in this connection, and the socialists are as innocent as the rest. Economics, indeed, has not at this point yet begun to take on a modern tone, unless the current neglect·of value theory by the socialists be taken as a negative symptom of advance, indicating that they at least recognize the futility of the received problems and solutions, even if they are not ready to make a positive move.

The shifting of the current point of view, from romantic philosophy to matter-of-fact, has affected the attitude of the Marxists towards the several articles of theory more than it has induced an avowed alteration or a substitution of new elements of theory for the old. It is always possible to make one's peace with a new standpoint by new interpretations and a shrewd use of figures of speech, so far as the theoretical formulation is concerned, and something of this kind has taken place in the case of Marxism; but when, as in the case of Marxism, the formulations of theory are drafted into practical use, substantial changes of appreciable magnitude are apt to show themselves in a changed attitude towards practical questions. The Marxists have had to face certain practical problems, especially problems of party tactics, and the substantial changes wrought in their theoretical outlook have come into evidence here. The real gravity of the changes that have overtaken Marxism would scarcely be seen by a scrutiny of the formal professions of the Marxists alone. But the exigencies of a changing situation have provoked readjustments of the received doctrinal position, and the shifting of the philosophical standpoint and postulates has come into evidence as marking the limits of change in their professions which the socialistic doctrinaires could allow themselves.

The changes comprised in the cultural movement that lies between the middle and the close of the nineteenth century are great and grave, at least as seen from so near a standpoint as the present day, and it is safe to say that, in whatever historical perspective they may be seen, they must, in some respects, always assert themselves as unprecedented. So far as concerns the present topic, there are three main lines of change that have converged upon the Marxist system of doctrines, and have led to its latter-day modification and growth. One of these -- the change in the postulates of knowledge, in the metaphysical foundations of theory -- has been spoken of already, and its bearing on the growth of socialist theory has been indicated in certain of its general features. But, among the circumstances that have conditioned the growth of the system, the most obvious is the fact that since Marx's time his doctrines have come to serve as the platform of a political movement, and so have been exposed to the stress of practical party politics dealing with a new and changing situation. At the same time the industrial (economic) situation to which the doctrines are held to apply - of which they are the theoretical formulation -- has also in important respects changed its character from what it was when Marx first formulated his views. These several lines of cultural change affecting the growth of Marxism cannot be held apart in so distinct a manner as to appraise the work of each separately. They belong inextricably together, as do the effects wrought by them in the system.

In practical politics the Social Democrats have had to make up their account with the labor movement, the agricultural population, and the imperialistic policy. On each of these heads the preconceived program of Marxism has come in conflict with the run of events, and on each head it has been necessary to deal shrewdly and adapt the principles to the facts of the time. The adaptation to circumstances has not been altogether of the nature of the compromise, although here and there the spirit of compromise and conciliation is visible enough. A conciliatory party policy may, of course, impose an adaptation of form and color upon the party principles. whether thereby seriously affecting the substance of the principles themselves; but the need of a conciliatory policy may, even more, provoke a substantial change of attitude toward practical questions in a case where a shifting of the theoretical point of view makes room for a substantial change.

Apart from all merely tactical expedients, the experience of the past thirty years has led the German Marxists to see the facts of the labor situation in a new light, and has induced them to attach an altered meaning to the accepted formulations of doctrine. The facts have not freely lent themselves to the scheme of the Marxist system, but the scheme has taken on such a new meaning as would be consistent with the facts. The untroubled Marxian economics, such as it finds expression in the Kapital and earlier documents of the theory, has no place and no use for a trade-union movement, or, indeed, for any similar non-political organization among the working class, and the attitude of the Social-Democratic leaders of opinion in the early days of the party's history was accordingly hostile to any such movement,15 -- as much so, indeed, as the loyal adherents of the classical political economy. That was before the modern industrial era had got under way in Germany, and therefore before the German socialistic doctrinaires had learned by experience what the development of industry was to bring with it. It was also before the modern scientific postulates had begun to disintegrate the neo-Hegelian preconceptions as to the logical sequence in the development of institutions.

In Germany, as elsewhere, the growth of the capitalistic system presently brought on trade-unionism; that is to say, it brought on an organized attempt on the part of the workmen to deal with the questions of capitalistic production and distribution by business methods, to settle the problems of working-class employment and livelihood by a system of nonpolitical, businesslike bargains. But the great point of all socialist aspiration and endeavor is the abolition of all business and all bargaining, and, accordingly, the Social Democrats were heartily out of sympathy with the unions and their endeavors to make business terms with the capitalist system, and make life tolerable for the workmen under that system. But the union movement grew to be so serious a feature of the situation that the socialists found themselves obliged to deal with unions, since they could not deal with the workmen over the heads of the unions. The Social Democrats, and therefore the Marxian theorists, had to deal with a situation which included the union movement, and this movement was bent on improving the workman's conditions of life from day to day. Therefore it was necessary to figure out how the union movement could and must further the socialistic advance; to work into the body of doctrines a theory of how the unions belong in the course of economic development that leads up to socialism, and to reconcile the unionist efforts at improvement with the ends of Social Democracy. Not only were the unions seeking improvement by unsocialistic methods, but the level of comfort among the working classes was in some respects advancing, apparently as a result of these union efforts. Both the huckstering animus of the workmen in their unionist policy and the possible amelioration of working-class conditions had to be incorporated into the socialistic platform and into the Marxist theory of economic development. The Marxist theory of progressive misery and degradation has, accordingly, fallen into the background, and a large proportion of the Marxists have already come to see the whole question of working-class deterioration in some such apologetic light as is shed upon it by Goldscheid in his Verelendungs-oder Meliorationstheorie. It is now not an unusual thing for orthodox Marxists to hold that the improvement of the conditions of the working classes is a necessary condition to the advance of the socialistic cause, and that the unionist efforts at amelioration must be furthered as a means toward the socialistic consummation. It is recognized that the socialistic revolution must be carried through not by an anaemic working class under the pressure of abject privation, but by a body of fullblooded workingmen gradually gaining strength from improved conditions of life. Instead of the revolution being worked out by the leverage of desperate misery, every improvement in working-class conditions is to be counted as a gain for the revolutionary forces. This is a good Darwinism, but it does not belong in the neo-Hegelian Marxism.

Perhaps the sorest experience of the Marxist doctrinaires has been with the agricultural population. Notoriously, the people of the open country have not taken kindly to socialism. No propaganda and no changes in the economic situation have won the sympathy of the peasant farmers for the socialistic revolution. Notoriously, too, the large-scale industry has not invaded the agricultural field, or expropriated the small proprietors, in anything like the degree expected by the Marxist doctrinaires of a generation ago. It is contained in the theoretical system of Marx that, as modern industrial and business methods gain ground, the small proprietor farmers will be reduced to the ranks of the wage-proletariat, and that, as this process of conversion goes on, in the course of time the class interest of the agricultural population will throw them into the movement side by side with the other wage-workmen.16 But at this point the facts have hitherto not come out in consonance with the Marxist theory. And the efforts of the Social Democrats to convert the peasant population to socialism have been practically unrewarded. So it has come about that the political leaders and the keepers of the doctrines have, tardily and reluctantly, come to see the facts of the agrarian situation in a new light, and to give a new phrasing to the articles of Marxian theory that touch on the fortunes of the peasant farmer. It is no longer held that either the small properties of the peasant farmer must be absorbed into larger properties, and then taken over by the State, or that they must be taken over by the State directly, when the socialistic revolution is established. On the contrary, it is now coming to be held that the peasant proprietors will not be disturbed in their holdings by the great change. The great change is to deal with capitalistic enterprise, and the peasant farming is not properly "capitalistic." It is a system of production in which the producer normally gets only the product of his own labor. Indeed, under the current régime of markets and credit relations, the small agricultural producer, it is held, gets less than the product of his own labor, since the capitalistic business enterprises with which he has to deal are always able to take advantage of him. So it has become part of the overt doctrine of socialists that as regards the peasant farmer it will be the consistent aim of the movement to secure him in the untroubled enjoyment of his holding, and free him from the vexatious exactions of his creditors and the ruinous business traffic in which he is now perforce involved. According to the revised code, made possible by recourse to Darwinian concepts of evolution instead of the Hegelian three-phase dialectic, therefore, and contrary to the earlier prognostications of Marx, it is no longer held that agricultural industry must go thru the capitalistic mill, and it is hoped that under the revised code it may be possible to enlist the interest and sympathy of this obstinately conservative element for the revolutionary cause. The change in the official socialist position on the agricultural question has come about only lately, and is scarcely yet complete, and there is no knowing what degree of success it may meet with either as a matter of party tactics or as a feature of the socialistic theory of economic development. All discussions of party policy, and of theory so far as bears on policy, take up the question; and nearly all authoritative spokesmen of socialism have modified their views in the course of time on this point.

The socialism of Karl Marx is characteristically inclined to peaceable measures and disinclined to a coercive government and belligerent politics. It is, or at least it was, strongly averse to international jealousy and patriotic animosity, and has taken a stand against armaments, wars, and dynastic aggrandizement. At the time of the French-Prussian war the official organization of Marxism, the International, went so far in its advocacy of peace as to urge the soldiery on both sides to refuse to fight. After the campaign had warmed the blood of the two nations, this advocacy of peace made the International odious in the eyes of both French and Germans. War begets patriotism, and the socialists fell under the reproach of not being sufficiently patriotic. After the conclusion of the war, the Socialistic Workingmen's Party of Germany sinned against the German patriotic sentiment in a similar way and with similarly grave results. Since the foundation of the empire and of the Social-Democratic party, the socialists and their doctrines have passed thru a further experience of a similar kind, but on a larger scale and more protracted. The government has gradually strengthened its autocratic position at home, increased its warlike equipment, and enlarged its pretensions in international politics, until what would have seemed absurdly impossible a generation ago is now submitted to by the German people, not only with a good grace, but with enthusiasm. During all this time that part of the population that has adhered to the socialist ideals has also grown gradually more patriotic and more loyal, and the leaders and keepers of socialist opinion have shared in the growth of chauvinism with the rest of the German people. But at no time have the socialists been able to keep abreast of the general upward movement in this respect. They have not attained the pitch of reckless loyalty that animates the conservative German patriots, although it is probably safe to say that the Social Democrats of to-day are as good and headlong patriots as the conservative Germans were a generation ago. During all this period of the new era of German political life the socialists have been freely accused of disloyalty to the national ambition, of placing their international aspirations above the ambition of imperial aggrandizement.

The socialist spokesmen have been continually on the defensive. They set out with a round opposition to any considerable military establishment, and have more and more apologetically continued to oppose any "undue" extension of the warlike establishments and the warlike policy. But with the passage of time and the habituation to warlike politics and military discipline, the infection of jingoism has gradually permeated the body of Social Democrats, until they have now reached such a pitch of enthusiastic loyalty as they would not patiently hear a truthful characterization of. The spokesmen now are concerned to show that, while they still stand for international socialism, consonant with their ancient position, they stand for national aggrandizement first and for international comity second. The relative importance of the national ad the international ideals in German socialist professions has been reversed since the seventies.17 The leaders are busy with interpretation of their earlier formulations. They have come to excite themselves over nebulous distinctions between patriotism and jingoism. The Social Democrats have come to be German patriots first and socialists second, which comes to saving that they are a political party working for the maintenance of the existing order, with modifications. They are no longer a party of revolution, but of reform, tho the measure of reform which they demand greatly exceeds the Hohenzollern limit of tolerance. They are now as much, if not more, in touch with the ideas of English liberalism than with those of revolutionary Marxism.

The material and tactical exigencies that have grown out of changes in the industrial system and in the political situation, then, have brought on far-reaching changes of adaptation in the position of the socialists. The change may not be extremely large at any one point, so far as regards the specific articles of the program, but, taken as a whole, the resulting modification of the socialistic position is a very substantial one. The process of change is, of course, not yet completed, -- whether or not it ever will be, but it is already evident that what is taking place is not so much a change in amount or degree of conviction on certain given points as a change in kind, - a change in the current socialistic habit of mind.

The factional discrepancies of theory that have occupied the socialists of Germany for some years past are evidence that the conclusion, even a provisional conclusion, of the shifting of their standpoint has not been reached. It is even hazardous to guess which way the drift is setting. It is only evident that the past standpoint, the standpoint of neo-Hegelian Marxism, cannot be regained, -- it is a forgotten standpoint. For the immediate present the drift of sentiment, at least among the educated, seems to set toward a position resembling that of the National Socials and the Rev. Mr. Naumann; that is to say, imperialistic liberalism. Should the conditions, political, social, and economic, which to-day are chiefly effective in shaping the habits of thought among the German people, continue substantially unchanged and continue to be the chief determining causes, it need surprise no one to find German socialism gradually changing into a somewhat characterless imperialistic democracy. The imperial policy seems in a fair way to get the better of revolutionary socialism, not by repressing it, but by force of the discipline in imperialistic ways of thinking to which it subjects all classes of the population. How far a similar process of sterilization is under way, or is likely to overtake the socialist movement in other countries, is an obscure question to which the German object-lesson affords no certain answer.

Notes:

1. "Scientific" is here used in the half technical sense which by usage it often has in this connection, designating the theories of Marx and his followers.

2. There is, indeed, a remarkable consistency, amounting substantially to an invariability of position, in Marx's writing, from the Communist Manifesto to the last volume of the Capital. The only portion of the great Manifesto which became antiquated, in the apprehension of its creators, is the polemics addressed to the Philosophical" socialists of the forties and the illustrative material taken from contemporary politics. The main position and the more important articles of theory, the materialistic conception, the doctrine of class struggle, the theory of value and surplus value, of increasing distress, of the reserve army, of the capitalistic collapse are to be found in the Critique of Political Economy (1859), and much of them in the Misery of Philosophy (1847), together with the masterful method of analysis and construction which he employed throughout his theoretical work.

3. Cf. Engels, Feuerbach (English translation, Chicago, 1903), especially Part IV., various papers published in the Neue Zeit; also the preface to the Communist Manifesto written in 1888; also the preface to volume II of Capital, where Engels argues the question of Marx's priority in connection with the leading theoretical principles of his system.

4. Cf. Feuerbach, as above; The Development of Socialism from Utopia to Science, especially sections II and III.

5. Such a socialist as Anton Menger, e.g., comes into the neo-Marxian school from without, from the field of modern scientific inquiry, and shows, at least virtually, no Hegelian color, whether in the scope of his inquiry, in his method, or in the theoretical work which he puts forth. It should be added that his Neue Staatslehre and Neue Sittenlehre are the first socialistic constructive work of substantial value as a

contribution to knowledge, outside of economic theory proper, that has appeared since Lassalle. The efforts of Engels (Ursprung der Familie) and Bebel (Der Frau) would scarcely be taken seriously as scientific monographs even by hot-headed socialists if it were not for the lack of anything better. Menger's work is not Marxism, whereas Engels' and Bebel's work of this class is practically without value or originality. The unfitness of the Marxian postulates and methods for the purposes of modern science shows itself in the sweeping barrenness of socialistic literature all along that line of inquiry into the evolution of institutions for the promotion of which the materialistic dialectic was invented.

6. This contrast holds between the original Marxism of Marx and the scope and method of modern science; but it does not, therefore, hold between the latterday Marxists -- who are largely imbued with post-Darwinian concepts -- and the non-Marxian scientists. Even Engels, in his latter-day formulation of Marxism is strongly affected with the notions of post-Darwinian science, and reads Darwinism into Hegel and Marx with a good deal of naivete. (See his Feuerbach, especially pp. 93-98 of the English translation.) So, also, the serious but scarcely quite consistent qualification of the materialistic conception offered by Engels in the letters printed in the Sozialistische Akademiker, 1895.

7. The fact that the theoretical structures of Marx collapse when their elements are converted into the terms of modern science should of itself be sufficient proof that those structures were not built by their maker out of such elements as modern science habitually makes use of. Marx was neither ignorant, imbecile, nor disingenuous, and his work must be construed from such a point of view and in terms of such elements as will enable his results to stand substantially sound and convincing.

8. Cf. Voraussetzungen des Sozialismus, especially the first two (critical) chapters. Bernstein's reverent attitude toward Marx and Engels, as well as his somewhat old-fashioned conception of the scope and method of science, gives his discussion an air of much greater consonance with the orthodox Marxism than it really has. In his latter expressions this consonance and conciliatory animus show up more strongly rather than otherwise. (See Socialism and Science, including the special preface written for the French edition.) That which was to Marx and Engels the point of departure and the guiding norm -- the Hegelian dialectic -- is to Bernstein a mistake from which scientific socialism must free itself. He says, e.g., (Voraussetzungen, end of ch. iv.), "The great things achieved by Marx and Engels they have achieved not by the help of the Hegelian dialectic, but in spite of it."
    The number of the "revisionists" is very considerable, and they are plainly gaining ground as against the Marxists of the older line of orthodoxy. They are by no means agreed among themselves as to details, but they belong together by virtue of their endeavor to so construe (and amend) the Marxian system as to bring it into consonance with the current scientific point of view. One should rather say points of view, since the revisionist endeavors are not all directed to bringing the received views in under a single point of view. There are two main directions of movement among the revisionists: (a) those who, like Bernstein, Conrad Schmidt, Tugan-Baronowski, Labriola, Ferri, aim to bring Marxism abreast of the standpoint of modern science, essentially Darwinists; and (b) those who aim to return to some footing on

the level of romantic philosophy. The best type and the strongest of the latter class are the neo-Kantians, embodying that spirit of revulsion to romantic norms of theory that makes up the philosophical side of the reactionary movement fostered by the discipline of German imperialism. (See K. Vorlander, Die neukantische Bewegung im Sozialismus.)

Except that he is not officially inscribed in the socialist calender, Sombart might be cited as a particularly effective revisionist, so far as concerns the point of modernizing Marxism and putting the modernized materialistic conception to work.

9. Cf. the files of the Neue Zeit, particularly during the controversy with Bernstein, and Bernstein und das Sozialdemokratische Programm.

10. The "idealist" socialists are even more in evidence outside of Germany. They may fairly be said to be in the ascendant in France, and they are a very strong and free-spoken contingent of the socialist movement of America. They do not commonly speak the language either of science or of philosophy, but, so far as their contentions may be construed from the standpoint of modern science, their drift seems to be something of the kind indicated above. At the same time the spokesmen of this scattering and shifting group stand for a variety of opinions and aspirations that cannot be classified under Marxism, Darwinism, or any other system of theory. At the margin they shade off into theology and the creeds.

11. Throughout the revisionist literature in Germany there is visible a softening of the traits of the doctrine of the class struggle, and the like shows itself in the programs of the party. Outside of Germany the doctrinaire insistence on this tenet is weakening even more decidedly. The opportunist politicians, with strong aspirations, but with relatively few and ill-defined theoretical preconceptions, are gaining ground.

12. Cf. Bernstein, Die heutige Sozialdemokratie in Theorie und Praxis, an answer to Brunhuber, Die heutige Sozialdemokratie, which should be consulted in the same connection; Goldscheid, Verelendungs- oder Meliorationstheorie; also Sombart, Sozialismus und soziale Bewegung, 5th edition, pp. 86-89.

13. Accordingly, in later Marxian handling of the questions of exploitation and accumulation, the attention is centred on the "surplus product" rather than on the "surplus value". It is also currently held that the doctrines and practical consequences which Marx derived from the theory of surplus value would remain substantially well founded, even if the theory of surplus value were given up. These secondary doctrines could be saved -- at the cost of orthodoxy -- by putting a theory of surplus product in the place of the theory of surplus value, as in effect is done by Bernstein (Sozialdemokratie in Theorie und Praxis, sec. 5. Also various essays included in Zur Geschichte und Theorie des Sozialismus).

14. The "right to the full product of labor" and the Marxian theory of exploitation associated with that principle has fallen into the background, except as a campaign cry designed to stir the emotions of the working class. Even as a campaign cry it has not the prominence, nor apparently the efficacy, which it once had. The tenet is better preserved, in fact, among the

"idealists", who draw for their antecedents on the French Revolution and the English philosophy of natural rights, than among the latter-day Marxists.

15. It is, of course, well known that even in the transactions and pronunciamentos of the International a good word is repeatedly said for the trade-unions, and both the Gotha and the Erfurt programs speak in favor of labor organizations, and put forth demands designed to further the trade-union endeavors. But it is equally well known that these expressions were in good part perfunctory, and that the substantial motive behind them was the politic wish of the socialists to conciliate the unionists, and make use of the unions for the propaganda. The early expressions of sympathy with the unionist cause were made for an ulterior purpose. Later on, in the nineties, there comes a change in the attitude of the socialist leaders toward the unions.

16. Cf. Capital, vol. i. ch. xiii., sect. 10.

17. Cf. Kautsky, Erfurter Programm, ch. v., sect. 13; Bernstein, Voraussetzungern, ch. iv., sect. e.

Lightning Source UK Ltd.
Milton Keynes UK
UKOW06f1846140617

303294UK00006B/611/P